Rules and Laws

by Graciela Vidal

Table of Contents

What Is a Rule?

A rule helps you know what you can or cannot do. There are rules at home, in school, and in the community.

Parents set the rules at home. They teach us to follow the rules. One rule at home could be washing your hands before eating.

▲ Parents teach their children the rules at the table.

In school students take turns listening to one another. They ask and answer questions.

▼ These children know how to take turns.

4

On the playground one rule is to treat everyone with respect.

▼ These children are following the playground rules.

5

There are rules in the library too. Everyone should talk softly inside the library. That is so we don't disturb others who are working or reading.

▼ These children are working quietly.

CHAPTER 2

How Do Rules Help Us?

Rules help protect us. The crossing guard helps us cross the street. It's a rule to wait until he tells us that we can go.

▲ The crossing guard stops the traffic, and the children safely cross the street.

There are rules on the school bus. You should sit in your seat. You can stand up only when the bus stops.

▼ These children obey the school bus rules.

There are rules at the pool. You should go to the pool with an adult. When you swim, make sure an adult is nearby.

▼ The mother and daughter are following the rules of the pool.

9

Recycling is a rule. It protects the planet. We recycle to keep Earth clean.

▼ Children can help protect the planet.

CHAPTER 3

What Is a Law?

A law is a rule made by the government. Many laws are made to keep us safe. Laws are for everyone.

▼ This boy wears a helmet to ride his bicycle. It's the law.

If you ride in a car wear a seat belt. It is the law.

▲ The seat belt protects you.

When children get on or off the school bus, all the traffic must stop. It is the law.

Cars and trucks must stop when the traffic light is red. They go when the light is green. That is another law.

▲ The driver waits until the light is green.

We must all respect other people's property. People should not take things that don't belong to them. That is the law.

▲ One law says not to take things without permission.

15

Rules and laws are important. They help protect everyone.